Monstrous Acts

a play by Steven Dawson

I0449243

Monstrous Acts

a play by Steven Dawson

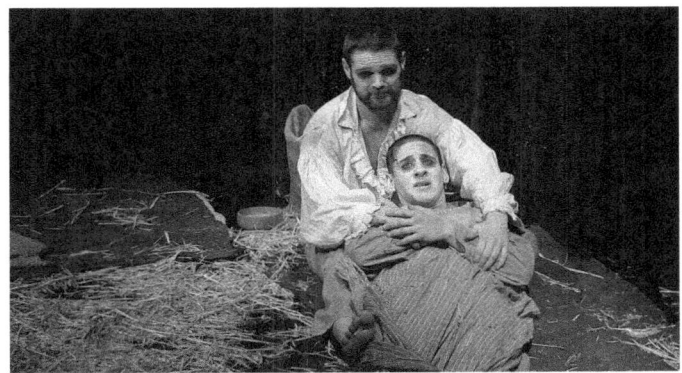

Kevin Dee & Mathew Gelsumini - Edinburgh Fringe 2012

Out Cast Theatre 2015

First Printing: 2015

ISBN 978-1-326-15376-2

Out Cast Theatre
PO Box 77
Craigieburn, VIC, AUSTRALIA 3064

www.outcast.org.au

Any application for performance must be made to:

RICK RAFTOS MANAGEMENT
P.O. Box 445, Paddington, NSW, Australia, 2021
raftos@raftos.com.au
Ph:(+612) 9281 9622 Fax:(+612) 9212 7100

Front Cover Photography by James Penlidis

Dedication

This play script is dedicated to the fearless courage of my two actors Antony Talia and Mathew Gelsumini without whom this project would never have happened. Their unflinching support, inspiration and commitment to the daunting task which lay ahead made the writing of this work a joy. Thanks guys.

S.D.

This play was first performed Oct 11th 2011
Mechanics Institute Performing Arts Centre Melbourne, Australia

Cast
Sebastian Mathew Gelsumini
Gilles   Antony Talia

Designed & Directed by Steven Dawson
Produced by Adrian Corbett & Out Cast Theatre

Mathew Gelsumini & Antony Talia - Out Cast Theatre 2011

MONSTROUS ACTS
A PLAY BY STEVEN DAWSON

SCENE ONE

LIGHTS UP ON A DINGY CELL. SEBASTIAN IS CROUCHED NAKED ON THE GROUND OVER A BUCKET WASHING HIMSELF WITH A RAG IT IS ALMOST BALLETIC IN MOVEMENT. A SHAFT OF MOONLIGHT BATHES ACROSS THE CELL. HE GETS UP AND STAGGERS ACROSS THE ROOM TO HIS BEDDING WITH A VERY PRONOUNCED LIMP AS IF INJURED. HE SLOWLY PUTS ON SOME RAGS FOR CLOTHES AND CURLS UP ON HIS BEDDING.

BLACKOUT

LIGHTS UP. SEBASTIAN IS CRYING. AFTER A MOMENT HE TAKES OUT A SMALL PIECE OF SHIMMERING CLOTH. HE WAVES IT THROUGH THE AIR. HE MOVES ACROSS THE CELL LIFTING AND ALLOWING THE CLOTH TO FLOAT AND DROP. HE DRAPES IT ACROSS HIS HEAD. HE BREATHES INTO IT. HE LOOKS UP THROUGH IT AND THEN TIGHTLY WRAPS IT AROUND HIS HEAD AS IF TO SUFFOCATE HIMSELF.

BLACKOUT

LIGHTS COME UP. SEBASTIAN SITS ON HIS BEDDING EATING SCRAPS FROM A TIN PLATE. VERY SLOWLY HE LOOKS AT THE FOOD, THE CURVES AND FEEL OF IT, BEFORE HE EATS IT AS IF EATING WAS SECONDARY.

BLACKOUT

LIGHTS UP. SEBASTIAN IS HUDDLED OVER HIMSELF IN THE CORNER OF HIS CELL. HE IS MASTURBATING FURIOUSLY. HE

WHIMPERS THEN SLIDES ACROSS HIS BEDDING AND BREATHES HEAVILY BEFORE FALLING ASLEEP.

BLACKOUT

LIGHTS UP ON SEBASTIAN SLEEPING. ANOTHER MAN, GILLES STANDS TO THE SIDE, ALSO IN FILTHY BUT MORE STYLISH REMNANTS OF CLOTHING. GILLES STARES AT HIM SLEEPING.

BLACKOUT

LIGHTS UP. GILLES IS NOW ASLEEP IN HIS BEDDING. SEBASTIAN STANDS, WATCHING HIM. GILLES IS HAVING A NIGHTMARE. HE TOSSES HIS BLANKET AWAY FROM HIMSELF. SEBASTIAN HESITATES FOR A MOMENT THEN SLOWLY APPROACHES GILLES AND ATTEMPTS TO PUT THE BLANKET OVER THE OTHER MAN. GILLES AWAKENS, STARTLED, GETS UP AND GRABS SEBASTIANBY THE THROAT AND PUSHES HIM TOWARDS HIS OWN BEDDING.

BLACKOUT

NIGHT. GILLES LAYS NAKED ON HIS BEDDING WITH HIS FACE AWAY FROM SEBASTIAN WHO HAS HIS BLANKET OVER HIM. GILLES' BODY IS MOVING SLOWLY UP AND DOWN AS HE VERY SLOWLY MASTURBATES. SEBASTIAN SLOWLY AWAKENS AND WATCHES GILLES AS HE CLIMAXES BEFORE FALLING ASLEEP, SOBBING QUIETLY.

BLACKOUT

LIGHTS UP. THE MEN ARE EATING THE SCRAPS FROM THEIR PLATES. GILLES FINISHES HIS MEAL FIRST THEN STANDS AND MOVES TOWARDS SEBASTIAN. GILLES SNATCHES THE FOOD OFF SEBASTIAN'S PLATE AND GOES BACK TO HIS BEDDING AND

EATS IT RAVENOUSLY. SBEASTIAN LOOKS ON.

BLACKOUT

NIGHT. GILLES STANDS LOOKING AT SEBASTIAN ASLEEP. SUDDENLY HE LEAPS ONTO SEBASTIAN AND BASHES HIS HEAD INTO THE BEDDING. HE LEAPS ONTO HIM AND AFTER TEARING HIS TROUSERS AWAY HE RAPES HIM. SEBASTIAN TRIES TO CRY OUT BUT GILLES COVERS HIS MOUTH AND BEATS HIM.

BLACKOUT

LIGHTS UP. GILLES ASLEEP. SEBASTIAN GETS UP. BLOOD RUNS DOWN THE BACK OF HIS LEGS. HE LOOKS AT THE BLOOD ON HIS HAND THEN AT GILLES' SLEEPING FORM. HE WIPES THE BLOOD ON HIS PANTS THEN PICKING UP HIS FOOD TRAY, JUMPS ONTO GILLES AND BEATS HIM ACROSS THE HEAD VIOLENTLY AS THE LIGHTS FADE. GILLES SCREAMS IN PAIN. BLACKOUT

LIGHTS UP. DAY. THEY SIT ON THEIR RESPECTIVE BEDDING. THEY ARE EATING. BOTH HAVE AN APPLE ON THEIR PLATE. GILLES GETS UP AND MOVES TOWARDS SEBASTIAN. SEBASTIAN RAISES HIS PLATE AS A WARNING TO STAY AWAY. GILLES GOES BACK TO HIS BEDDING. AFTER A MOMENT GILLES ROLLS HIS APPLE TOWARDS SEBASTIAN. SEBASTIAN LOOKS UP.

GILLES
You are thin. You should eat more. *[SEBASTIAN TAKES A BITE]* If I am to fuck you again then I do not want to feel your bones against my rod.

SEBASTIAN ROLLS THE APPLE BACK TO HIM VIOLENTLY.

BLACKOUT

SCENE TWO

LIGHTS UP. GILLES IS CROUCHED BESIDE SEBASTIAN SLEEPING. GILLES BITES INTO HIS APPLE WHICH STARTLES SEBASTIAN AWAKE. GILLES HOLDS OUT HIS APPLE TO HIM. SEBASTIAN TURNS OVER DISGUSTED.

GILLES
You do not talk. That is good. There is far too much talking in the world. Are you a mute? *[SEBASTIAN SHAKES HIS HEAD]*So you just choose not to talk. It is a wise man who knows not to blow his bugle. You are angry with me still. This I understand. We know nothing of each other but already I have taken something from you that you would not willingly give up if not for the situation we find ourselves in. Or perhaps you would. I do not know you. *[PAUSE]* Why are you here? *[SEBASTIAN LOOKS AWAY]* It is of no matter. What you have done...what I have done...we all go to the same place soon enough. The past will favour us no more. Perhaps we go to hell. If there is a hell. I'm not so easily convinced. Most who know me will say I was born to it. Those who sat in judgment believe it to be my final destination. But who is to say this is not hell already and there will be something better beyond the veil. You already have the silence of the dead about you. Will there be a hell for you? No. For you the path is not so clear. Not to my mind. You have a complication about you, I think.

SEBASTIAN
What did you do?

GILLES
Ah. He does speak. Do?

SEBASTIAN
Why are you here? What did you do that I am to share your company?

GILLES
What is your name?

SEBASTIAN
Sebastian. Sebastian Richet.

GILLES
Well, Sebastian Richet, it is good to be in your acquaintance. My name is Gilles de Lavall. You may have heard of me.

SEBASTIAN
I have not. Answer me. What did you do?

GILLES
What I did, my friend, is to kill. What I have done to bring me *here* is a longer and more complicated tale and I do not think time allows the retelling to give my story full justice.

SEBASTIAN
You killed someone?

GILLES
You know nothing of me? I should be offended. The condemnation of my judges to my crimes had me believe my name would be mentioned in hushed tones right across France and beyond. The guards have told you nothing?

SEBASTIAN
They do not speak to me. I have not exchanged words with anyone in 3 months. They throw my food in and say nothing. They change my bucket and say nothing. The slot opens, the slot closes. They never check to see if I am dead. No words are exchanged.

GILLES
You have been here 3 months?

SEBASTIAN
I think so.

GILLES
You do not know?

SEBASTIAN
I came here in late autumn. I think it is now near winter's end? Yes?

GILLES
Yes.

SEBASTIAN
Then 3 months is close I think. It matters little anyway.

GILLES
I do not think I could live here for 3 months.

SEBASTIAN
Then it is just as well you are to die.

GILLES
If I were not the man I am I might be upset that you remark of my impending fate in such a cavalier fashion. Have you always been here by yourself?

SEBASTIAN
Yes. Who did you kill?

GILLES
You insist on knowing.

SEBASTIAN
You do not have to tell me.

GILLES
Perhaps later. When I am of a more amiable temper.

SEBASTIAN
A moment ago you were offended when I did not know who you were. Now you play coy with the detail of your exploits.

GILLES
Let us just say there was a miscarriage of justice.

SEBASTIAN
You are innocent then?

GILLES
I did not say that. But I am sure this prison is full of innocent men. What of you? What miscarriage of justice has placed you in my company?

SEBASTIAN
I was here first. A man died through my actions.

GILLES
So you were you the cause of another man's demise? I won't judge you.

SEBASTIAN
It was accidental.

GILLES
Most deaths are. But was it your fault?

SEBASTIAN
It was a tavern brawl. He fell against a fireplace hearth and struck his head. He died.

GILLES
You are very scant with the detail, my friend.

SEBASTIAN
Had I not pushed him there would be no crime. That is all there is to tell. No more.

GILLES
I hope your defence at trial was stronger than the telling of it.

SEBASTIAN
He was an aristocrat. I had no means to pay for a strong defence or any de- fence for that matter.

GILLES
For the lack of coin you are to die. There's seems little justice in this world.

SEBASTIAN
You appear to come from money yet the axe beckons you also.

GILLES
That is true. Money is little guarantee of a calm sailing. And your leg? It troubles you. Was this also part of the same accident?

SEBASTIAN
I am tired.

GILLES
Very well.

BLACKOUT

SCENE THREE

BOTH MEN WASH FROM THEIR RESPECTIVE BUCKETS IN A REPTITION OF THE SAME BALLETIC-TYPE MOVEMENT FROM

THE FIRST SCENE. THEY MIRROR EACH IN MOVEMENT AND ACTION AS THEY DRESS. ONCE DRESSED THEY LOOK AT EACH OTHER.

BLACKOUT

LIGHTS UP. SEBASTIAN IS HAVING A NIGHTMARE. HE CRIES OUT WHICH WAKENS GILLES. HE GETS UP AND MOVES TOWARDS SEBASTIAN AND STANDS WATCHING HIM FOR A MOMENT. HE MOVES AWAY, STOPS THEN RETURNS, CROUCHES DOWN BESIDE HIM AND PULLS THE BLANKET OVER SEBASTIAN'S SHOULDERS. HE BRUSHES HIS HAND ACROSS SEBASTIAN'S FOREHEAD WHICH CALMS HIM. AS HE STARTS TO MOVE AWAY SEBASTIAN GRABS HIS HAND AND HOLDS IT TO HIS FOREHEAD. GILLES LOOKS DOWN AT HIM AS THE LIGHTS FADE.

BLACKOUT.

SCENE FOUR

LIGHTS UP. THE MEN ARE EATING ON THEIR RESPECTIVE BEDS.

GILLES
This man you killed. Who was he?

SEBASTIAN
I did not know him or his name at the time.

GILLES
Then what was the fight about?

SEBASTIAN
He had made some comment reflecting upon the virtue of the woman serving him wine. I was quick to rage and he drew a knife. I deflected

his attack but in the melee he was mortally injured.

GILLES
Perhaps I am wrong but you do not strike me as the sort of person to frequent a tavern.

SEBASTIAN
It was my first and only visit.

GILLES
They often say wine will be the death of you.

SEBASTIAN
You mock me?

GILLES
I mock the circumstance of your imprisonment. I think you unjustly treated and the punishment not fitting but in these times balance of justice is heavily weighted in favour of those with means. Mere men and women are given short shrift.

SEBASTIAN
I think you are right.

GILLES
The aristocracy are above normal men for they are the ones who make the laws that enable them to continue their own lives in comfort and without hindrance.

SEBASTIAN
You are rich.

GILLES
That is a crass word. I am…was…very comfortable.

SEBASTIAN
And now no longer?

GILLES
Years of extravagance and bad business decisions had depleted my fortune. You may not think it but I was once one of the wealthiest men in France. Several castles and estates.

SEBASTIAN
All gone?

GILLES
All gone. The little remaining has been taken up by the state and the court.

SEBASTIAN
Why?

GILLES
Various claims against me that were ruled not in my favour. And the buying of silence in testimony can be very expensive even with peasants.

SEBASTIAN
No wife or parents to reign you in?

GILLES
Parents both dead and as for wife only briefly but none worth mentioning. Alas I had frittered away her fortune as well and she could take no more. She took to a convent and died soon after from I know not what.

SEBASTIAN
You do not mourn for her?

GILLES
All feeling for her had abated on our wedding night. She was but a means

to an end and was well aware of my nature. That is all to be said on the matter. What of you? A woman in your life?

SEBASTIAN
A wife I have not seen since my incarceration. She has made no attempt to visit that I know of and only briefly appeared at my trial.

GILLES
Like myself you must have married young and in haste.

SEBASTIAN
The wooing was brief. The love briefer still. To her *I* was the means to an end. She escaped her family and for a brief time I escaped loneliness.

GILLES
A prison is an odd place to speak about love.

SEBASTIAN
Perhaps.

GILLES
Do you read? I should have you read poems to ease our nights. Perhaps the prose of Alain Chartier. Are you familiar with his work? I have always thought him overrated and prone to whimsy.

SEBASTIAN
Now I know you mock me. I cannot read nor will I continue this line of conversation.

GILLES
I need you not to have conversation. I am quite happy talking to myself.

SEBASTIAN
Then they would think you mad and moved to an asylum or possessed and burnt for a heretic.

GILLES
Madness would not be enough to have my sentence revoked. My actions have all but proved that.

SEBASTIAN
And for heresy?

GILLES
The church is a bitter mistress. I would sooner beheading than burnt. I suppose it is the way of things. Our demise is nought but entertainment for the crowd.

SEBASTIAN
I do not think my death will draw the crowd.

GILLES
Never underestimate spectacle. The crowd will have its amusement come what may.

SEBASTIAN
I have not witnessed a burning.

GILLES
You are fortunate. I myself saw the Maid burnt. It was barbaric. Would that I had half her strength of character when I face death.

SEBASTIAN
You speak as if you knew her.

GILLES
I did but briefly know her in battle. An ignorant girl prone to fantasy but with such an unyielding grasp to her faith and vision. Visions sadly that blinded her to the machinations and corruption of clergy. It is strange for you remind me of her. You accept your fate without anger or reproach.

SEBASTIAN
I would know more of your life.

GILLES
If only to pass time? No. I know my life and the history of it. It is shabby, decadent and the telling would be boastful rambling. I would hear more of yours.

SEBASTIAN
There is little to tell. Both mother and father dead, blacksmith was my trade and until I came here I had not ventured far from my village. As you can see I have not your exploits to draw from.

GILLES
Ah but there is much I have done and so much more I do regret.

SEBASTIAN
You are very calm.

GILLES
Perhaps my days seem calm for I find some peace in talking to you but in sleep many voices I have wronged do cry out.

SEBASTIAN
I know sometimes darkness overcomes you for I have seen it.

GILLES
Enough! This conversation drags me to melancholy. I will have no more of it.

SEBASTIAN
I am sorry.

GILLES
You have nothing to be sorry about. I am quick to charge. That is my

nature and it is a burden. I would have my last days in this wretched world filled with happier thoughts. You should sleep.

THE LIGHTS FADE.

BLACKOUT

SCENE FIVE

LIGHTS COME UP ON SEBASTIAN WASHING HIMSELF SLOWLY NEAR HIS BUCKET IN THE SAME BALLETIC STYLE. GILLES SITS ON HIS BED WATCHING HIM. SEBASTIAN FEELS GILLES' EYES ON HIM. HE TURNS AWAY. GILLES STANDS UP AND GOES OVER TO HIM. HE TAKES THE RAG FROM SEBASTIAN. HE WETS IT AND STARTS TO WASH SEBASTIAN'S BODY SLOWLY. HE LEANS IN AND KISSES HIM SOFTLY ON THE LIPS. SEBASTIAN IS STUNNED. GILLES SLOWLY CONTINUES TO WASH SEBASTIAN'S BODY. HE DROPS TO THE FLOOR THEN KISSES SEBASTIAN'S INJURED LEG. QUICKLY HE EMBRACES SEBASTIAN AND SOBS AGAINST HIS LEG. SEBASTIAN LOOKS DOWN ON HM WITH PITY. HE LIFTS HIM UP THEN SLOWLY REMOVES GILLES' CLOTHES. HE TAKES THE RAG FROM GILLES AND STARTS TO WASH GILLES' BODY. THEY BOTH STAND IN CLOSE EMBRACE AND KISS AS THE LIGHTS FADE.

LIGHTS UP ON THE BED AS THE MEN WRITHE AND TWIST SLOWLY IN PASSION. GILLES IS LETTING SEBASTIAN PENETRATE HIM. THEY KISS PASSIONATELY AS THE LIGHTS FADE.

SCENE SIX

THEY LIE IN THE BED EMBRACING.

GILLES
You should thank me.

SEBASTIAN
Thank you?

GILLES
Of course. Now you will have two sins to atone for when you meet
your maker. A much more worthy score to be judged by.

SEBASTIAN
I see no sin. I see this as what it is.

GILLES
That argument holds little water with your church. I do not think we
will have much more of this.

SEBASTIAN
I know. Right now I care not.

GILLES
Very well.

SEBASTIAN
You did not enjoy it?

GILLES
Do you need me to tell you?

SEBASTIAN
No.

GILLES
Are you scared? Of dying?

SEBASTIAN
Are you?

GILLES
You do that quite a lot.

SEBASTIAN
What?

GILLES
Answer my question with another question.

SEBASTIAN
I was not aware of it.

GILLES
So? Do you fear death?

SEBASTIAN
I will myself to not think on it.

GILLES
In these circumstances it seems fitting to think of little else.

SEBASTIAN
It will come when it comes. I have no control over it. I leave no one behind that would mourn my loss.

GILLES
Nor I.

SEBASTIAN
I would mourn you.

GILLES
You would?

SEBASTIAN
Of course.

GILLES
I have behaved monstrously towards you.

SEBASTIAN
That is now past. It is what it is.

GILLES
You are too forgiving. And if your death precedes mine?

SEBASTIAN
Then you can mourn me.

GILLES
I will mourn our talks.

SEBASTIAN
That is something I suppose.

GILLES
You have not answered my question. Do you fear death?

SEBASTIAN
I think of the pain.

GILLES
Pain?

SEBASTIAN
When it happens.

GILLES
I am led to believe it happens so quick there is no pain.

SEBASTIAN
I have been told that people's eyes move when it happens.

GILLES
So?

SEBASTIAN
So if their eyes move then they are looking at something. If they are looking at something then they are thinking of that thing and if they are thinking of that thing then they must be thinking of other things also which means their mind is open to stimulation of some form and pain is a form of stimulation.

GILLES
Well I can attest to pain being a source of stimulation but I think you think too much on it. It will be a different feeling.

SEBASTIAN
In here I have nothing else to think about. Do you believe in heaven?

GILLES
That is a strange question. I asked you some time ago if you believed in hell and received no answer.

SEBASTIAN
I did not know you then.

GILLES
You think you know me now? You know only what you see before you and what I have told you. And of course our initial introduction was of a slightly different and I would guess entirely predictable nature given the circumstances.

SEBASTIAN
You do not have to answer me.

GILLES
Then you must answer me first. Do you believe in hell?

SEBASTIAN
Yes.

GILLES
Why? Because your church tells you there is a hell?

SEBASTIAN
It is your church too.

GILLES
My church abandoned me many years ago and I it. I have it on first-hand experience that men of the church are as debauched and depraved as the basest amongst us and more likely to commit sin than any other.

SEBASTIAN
You know this?

GILLES
I know this all too well.

SEBASTIAN
Christ will forgive us all. He will embrace you again if you ask.

GILLES
Oh would that that were true. I am afraid the level of my crimes is so great and my nature so unredeemable that even Christ could not be that forgiving.

SEBASTIAN
You say that in a boastful fashion. It must be a something extraordinary.

GILLES
It was something that overcame me. An urge that left me temporarily blind to any semblance of morality. I had become an animal. That is all I wish to say on the matter to you lest you change your opinion of me.

SEBASTIAN
What opinion must you think I have of you? And why would you care in any case?

GILLES
I don't know. I would perhaps have one person in the world who does not think me a monster.

SEBASTIAN
That is why we have parents I think. You will not tell me?

GILLES
No.

SEBASTIAN
I could ask the guards.

GILLES
You do not speak to them, remember?

SEBASTIAN
Of course. It would seem suspicious and strange to them that I sought conversation. They ignore me. Some days I am not fed. I think they would be happier if I were already dead. Before you came here I was the only in this part of the prison. Most others had been…dispatched already. Or sent to other gaols upon decree of clemency. Perhaps that will happen to you.

GILLES
I think not. Do you not think it odd that they should put you into the same cell as me when there are other cells that lay vacant.

SEBASTIAN
They are short on executioners.

GILLES
What?

SEBASTIAN
It is true. This is a small town. The resident executioner had to go to Rheims to clear a backlog. I think he was working alphabetically. He left before he got to me.

GILLES
You have a sense of humour. I was not aware of that.

SEBASTIAN
Perhaps they thought it easier to keep one cell clean and I might enjoy company before they lop my head off.

GILLES
Or they thought I would kill you and save them the effort.

SEBASTIAN
Perhaps.

PAUSE

GILLES
I wouldn't.

SEBASTIAN
I know that now.

THERE IS THE SOUND OF KEYS, A SMALL COUGH AND SHUFFLE FROM OUTSIDE THE CELL. THEY LOOK TOWARDS THE DOOR AS THE LIGHTS FADE.

BLACKOUT

SCENE SEVEN

THE SOUND OF SCREAMING AS THE LIGHTS COME UP ON GILLES WHO HAS JUST WOKEN. SEBASTIAN IS NOT IN THE CELL BUT HIS SCREAMS CAN BE HEARD OFF AS IF HE WERE BEING TORTURED.

GILLES
Sebastian! Sebastian!

HE CONTINUES TO CRY OUT TO HIM AS THE SCREAMS CONTINUE.

BLACKOUT

SCENE EIGHT

LIGHTS COME UP ON SEBASTIAN BEATEN AND BLOODY, COWERING IN THE CORNER. GILLES WAKENS AND RUSHES TO HIM AS SEBASTIAN MOANS AND CRIES IN PAIN. GILLES GATHERS HIM IN HIS ARMS AND TRIES TO COMFORT HIM AS THE LIGHTS FADE.

BLACKOUT

SCENE NINE

LIGHTS UP. GILLES KNEELS OVER THE BUCKET SLOWLY WASHING THE BLOOD FROM SEBASTIAN'S BODY.

GILLES
Why?

SEBASTIAN
I do not know. They said nothing. I cannot think myself worthy of a beating for my actions alone or they would have finished me off long ago. I can only think it was to get at you.

GILLES
By torturing you?

SEBASTIAN
I suspect they know we have become close.

GILLES
Then we must stop. I will not have you harmed for me.

SEBASTIAN
No.

GILLES
[GOING TO THE CELL DOOR AND SCREAMING] They are animals and cowards! Taking you whilst I slept. It makes little sense when we already go to our deaths.

HE GOES BACK AND TOUCHES SEBASTIAN'S LEG. HE RESPONDS IN MUCH PAIN.

GILLES
Your leg grows worse. I think it more than infection.

SEBASTIAN
They made sure they struck it several times.

GILLES
They have done this before?

SEBASTIAN
When first I came here. I was beaten harshly.

GILLES
I am sorry.

SEBASTIAN
You have no cause. It is they who wish us harm. That is all. It is in their nature.

GILLES
I know other forces would pay happily to cause me distress. Many enemies still seek revenge. You must forgive me. I will ask to be put in another cell.

SEBASTIAN
Why?

GILLES
So they should not trouble you again. I will not have you beaten for any- thing I have done. I curse them and their whoring mothers.

SEBASTIAN
You will not leave me.

GILLES
I must.

SEBASTIAN
You will not! Promise me.

GILLES
Sebastian...

SEBASTIAN
Promise!

GILLES
Very well. I shall not leave you. And if they come for you again?

SEBASTIAN
Then you must protect me.

GILLES
I will not sleep. You have my word.

SEBASTIAN
And I will hold you to it.

HE CONTINUES WIPING HIM AS THE LIGHTS FADE.

BLACKOUT

SCENE TEN

LIGHTS UP. SEBASTIAN LAYS SHIVERING IN THE CORNER, COVERED IN HIS BLANKET. GILLES WAKES.

GILLES
Sebastian? Sebastian!

SEBASTIAN
I am here.

HE GOES OVER TO HIM AND FEELS HIS FOREHEAD.

GILLES
To bed. You have fever. I fear the infection has spread. I keep telling you, you must rest. I should call the guards.

SEBASTIAN
You think they will come? You are more optimistic than I.

GILLES
I do not know what to do. Tell me what I must do.

SEBASTIAN
Do not fret so. I am stronger than I look. Just stay by me. Talk to me.

GILLES
Talk?

SEBASTIAN
I had been without company for so long. You think I grow tired of conversation?

GILLES
I think you do with me. I have nothing to tell you.

SEBASTIAN
That is true. You are a sealed box, are you not? Perhaps you can recite some of your learnt poetry. Do you know any?

GILLES
A little. But only fragments do I hold in my head.

SEBASTIAN
I would be satisfied with fragments.

GILLES
They are utterings. Meaningless in the circumstances.

SEBASTIAN
You should let me be the judge.

GILLES
Ah. Let me see.

I leave it to the lover, who nurses
Hopes that his wound might heal,
To make ballads, songs and verses,
That each might his own skill reveal
My lady, by her will, did steal
At her Death, God save her soul,
And carry away, my power to feel
That lies with her beneath the stone.

SEBASTIAN
[AFTER A PAUSE] You say I am the Lady?

GILLES
No. Of course not. It is but a fragment of a much larger work.

SEBASTIAN
What does it mean?

GILLES
I am not sure. A man hopes that though his love had died he will feel again?

SEBASTIAN
That is a very depressing work. I am unwell. Not dead. I think if I hear any more of that work I should be pushed to Death's door. You have nothing… lighter in your arsenal?

GILLES
I am no orator or court entertainment. I told you I know little.

SEBASTIAN
Then you must find other works fast and learn them robustly or your friends may desert you for more worthy entertainment.

GILLES
You rally to insult me.

SEBASTIAN
It is the way of things. You should not be surprised.

GILLES
Do you feel better?

SEBASTIAN
A little.

GILLES
We must get some food or broth for you. Or perhaps you would like an apple?

SEBASTIAN
I find that not amusing. Give me some more words.

GILLES
More words for you to mock me. Of course.

If any would constrain my will
To write of happy things,
My pen would not possess the skill
Nor my tongue the power to sing.
My lips could never part, in smiling,
Without a gaze that lips betrayed,
Since my heart would claim denial
Through the tears my cheeks displayed

SEBASTIAN
No. That has not done it. Your bedside manner fails you.

GILLES
Be quiet.

LIGHTS FADE

BLACKOUT

SCENE ELEVEN

SEBASTIAN WAKENS. GILLES STANDS BY THE DOOR.

SEBASTIAN
Gilles?

GILLES
Yes?

SEBASTIAN
I thought you gone.

GILLES
No.

SEBASTIAN
It is middle of the night I think. What has happened?

GILLES
I have been awake for hours. The guard has informed me the executioner visits at dawn.

SEBASTIAN
Dawn?

GILLES
Yes.

SEBASTIAN
I see. So soon. Is there any order to it?

GILLES
We will be taken to the square together. Then we ascend the scaffold. First you, then me.

SEBASTIAN
I hope it does not rain. That would be depressing. *[GILLES SAYS NOTHING]* Gilles?

GILLES
What?

SEBASTIAN
Our day draws near and you become distant? Why do you not share with me as we once did?

GILLES
I know. You have been unwell. I did not want to trouble you.

SEBASTIAN
The fever has passed but two days ago. Trouble me.

GILLES
You are still weak.

SEBASTIAN
I would make the most of what time we have.

GILLES
I see the dawn coming.

SEBASTIAN
It is still night. There is no birdsong. You should sleep.

GILLES
I am past sleep. There will be no more sleep for me. Sebastian, I am sorry.

SEBASTIAN
For what?

GILLES
You follow me soon enough yet all I think about is how *my* life will end.

SEBASTIAN
Calm. Calm yourself.

GILLES
I do not want to die. I lied before. I am not brave.

SEBASTIAN
You are braver than you know. I believe we all are.

GILLES
I believe you are but for all my bravery in battle of one kind or another I

still stand here before you a coward.

SEBASTIAN
You are no coward.

GILLES
Then why does my body shake? My throat run dry? My hands sweat?

SEBASTIAN
You must try to quiet your mind.

GILLES
I cannot think of anything other than that my end should bring my soul peace. But what peace will there be for me? I would have that peace now…that it were over.

SEBASTIAN
It will come soon enough my friend.

GILLES
I am a fool. I have left that which should be done undone.

SEBASTIAN
You have not done enough in your life?

GILLES
I must confess my crimes.

SEBASTIAN
You have admitted your guilt already.

GILLES
In the eyes of men. That is useless. I talk of my confession before God.

SEBASTIAN
Confess them to your priest when the time comes.

GILLES
I will have no priest. I have told them. But now I do regret that decision. It was made in defiance and haste.

SEBASTIAN
Then confess them to me.

GILLES
I cannot.

SEBASTIAN
Why?

GILLES
You know me of one way. I would not have you think otherwise of me.

SEBASTIAN
I know you more complicated than you outwardly show but you have also shown me that which I do admire in men. You have the capacity for much love.

GILLES
And the capability for such monstrous acts.

SEBASTIAN
Come. I will be your confessor. I will not judge you. I will listen and give you comfort.

GILLES
You do that already. I have worn out my welcome at your door.

SEBASTIAN
You have a good heart.

GILLES
A good heart?! You have no idea what I have done. You know me from this place only.

SEBASTIAN
You are angry with me?

GILLES
I am angry with the world.

SEBASTIAN
But the world is not here. It is a small cell and soon the walls will fall away.

GILLES
The world wants no more part of me.

SEBASTIAN
Then the world is a fool.

GILLES
You have the good heart. Not me. That the world of men would remove your light from it is blasphemous.

SEBASTIAN
And you are someone who would know blasphemy.

GILLES
Now you mock me?!

SEBASTIAN
You should try to sleep.

GILLES
Again with the sleep! Enough already!

SEBASTIAN
I am sorry.

GILLES
Do not be sorry. Help me!

SEBASTIAN
How?

GILLES
Take away this pain!

SEBASTIAN
I cannot! I do not know where your pain lies. Only that your guilt over- whelms you. *[PAUSE]* What is your confession?

GILLES
You must promise me you will not judge or think any less of me.

SEBASTIAN
You have shown me much love and care. I have not the right to rebuke or call you on it.

GILLES
Promise me!

SEBASTIAN
I promise.

GILLES
You think I go to my death on a single count. I have killed not one man. I have taken the lives of many.

SEBASTIAN
If it be in battle then the cause is just.

GILLES
This was no battle. Unless the battle is with evil itself and for some years I am taken its prisoner and was coerced into service. I have had a sickness inside of me that until most but 6 months ago did fester and infect.

SEBASTIAN
What sickness? Tell me. What have you done?

GILLES
I killed so many. So many children.

SEBASTIAN
Children?

GILLES
I am a murderer of boys. There were some girls but mostly boys. Over 200 saw their deaths directly or indirectly at my hands. I acted not alone. Others aided by fear of death, removal from my company and loss of land and income. Field hands and servants were oft my agents to entice many victims to my estates where they were fed then soon after debauched, robbed of their innocence and then dispatched sometimes with nauseating frenzy by myself or likeminded company. Some as young as 10 years. Young village boys come a'begging at my door were never seen by their parents again, their bones flamed the fires in many of my kitchens and those who knew were justly frightened that to speak of it would see them quickly dispatched in one gruesome way or another by myself or those in my service. It was a sickness that overwhelmed me to such a degree that there were times when I would bathe in the bloodied entrails of a beautiful youth. Cutting their limbs away would bring me to arousal and ecstasy. Only on hearing their screams as I plunged my erect member into a newly created wound

would it leave me satiated. Were it not for my arrogance and the betrayal by some of my co-conspirators in giving testimony against I would still be at large to continue this perversion. They are now dead for all their bargaining and I am to soon follow. Be assured I am not of that inclination now. It was a madness that o'er took me or a dark hand that guides many men to do evil upon others. It is the story of my last few years and this is the man you share your last hours with. You now see my reluctance to talk on it.

SEBASTIAN
No more! I can hear no more of this! If only part of the story bears truth what you have told me chills my soul. This is not the person I lay with and found comfort with. Who tendered to me when I was weakened and showed great compassion, more telling than the doorway of some convent. The tale you tell is of a madman. Not of this earth. I do believe you have been visited by the devil and that he will indeed seek your company again in the afterlife. You may burn as you feared but for your crimes it will be eternity.

GILLES
You said you would only hear the story of it.

SEBASTIAN
But this goes beyond. I have difficulty in fathoming the detail of it. You must allow me a moment. Why? Why did this happen?

GILLES
I know not how the urge devoured me. Only that it did.

SEBASTIAN
This sends my head reeling.

GILLES
Do not judge me! I could not bear that from you. You are all that is good in my ever diminishing world. Remove your affection from me and I go

to my death with nought.

SEBASTIAN
I will not judge you. That will come from one greater than us all. I have pity for you. *[HE PAUSES]* just as I have pity for the souls of those you have taken.

GILLES
You still think that a just God exists? A God that would allow such a creature as I to flourish under his gaze?

SEBASTIAN
I do believe! Just as I do believe you that you believe He exists. Otherwise you would not fear His judgment so. You are no heretic.

GILLES
If there were a just God you would not be here.

SEBASTIAN
We are hours from our deaths and now you question His existence?

GILLES
I question His motives. For He has failed so many. Those who fall in battle, those whose lives I took and your torture and removal from this world for a mere accident…and I want the voices that cry out in my sleep to cease. I want to be free of this anguish.

SEBASTIAN
It will come.

GILLES
But with such finality. *[HE LOOKS AT SEBASTIAN]* I would have my life over again. To meet you again. To shower you with the love you deserve and reveal to you a world much brighter for your place in it.

HE STANDS SOBBING. FINALLY SEBASTIAN GOES TO HIM AND WRAPS HIM IN HIS ARMS AS GILLES SOBS.

SEBASTIAN
Before the end you will find your strength. Be assured. Even at our weakest we can be strong. Come. Lie with me once more. You must sleep.

GILLES
I cannot. Stay awake with me.

SEBASTIAN
I will stay awake with you as long as you need me.

GILLES
You will not fall asleep?

SEBASTIAN
I will not.

GILLES
I am sorry for all I have done to you.

SEBASTIAN
You have done for me more than you know. You have my heart. I will not leave you.

GILLES FALLS ASLEEP IN SEBASTIAN'S ARMS AS SEBASTIAN STROKES GILLES' HAIR. WHEN HE IS ASLEEP SEBASTIAN SLOWLY REACHES BEHIND AND TAKES OUT THE CLOTH HE HAS KEPT HIDDEN. WITH ONE HAND HE ROLLS IT IN A BALL, GENTLEY OPENS GILLES MOUTH AS HE SLEEPS AND PUTS THE CLOTH INSIDE HIS MOUTH. GILLES WAKENS THEN STRUGGLES AS SEBASTIAN COVERS GILLES' NOSE AND SUFFOCATES HIM. GILLES CONTINUES TO STRUGGLE TRYING TO FIGHT HIM OFF.

SEBASTIAN HOLDS FAST LOOKING ON HIM WITH LOVE. AFTER A WHILE GILLES RELAXES UNTIL ALL BREATH IS GONE. SEBASTIAN TAKES THE CLOTH OUT OF HIS MOUTH, WEEPS AND KISSES HIM GENTLY.

SEBASTIAN
There. Now sleep. You have nothing to fear now. No more pain. The voices are gone. You are at peace and all is ended. I shall see you again, my friend.

HE SOBS AS THE LIGHTS FADE ON THEM BOTH.

BLACKOUT

LIGHTS COME UP ON STAIRS AS SEBASTIAN MAKES HIS WAY TOWARDS A BLOCK WITH AN AXE EMBEDDED IN IT. HE LOOKS AT THE AXE THEN TOWARDS THE CELL THEN SKYWARDS TOWARDS SUNRISE.

BLACKOUT

END